THE STRONG MEN WE NEED

TO BUILD STRONG SONS, STRONG DAUGHTERS, AND STRONG HOMES

JOHN M. O'MALLEY

OMALLEY
BOOKS.COM

To John, my son, Sydney's Father, and Hannah's Husband

CONTENTS

HOW TO USE THIS BOOK

How to Use This Book

The Strong Men We Need is a 31-day devotional journey written for Christian men who want to grow in biblical manhood. Whether you're reading this on your own, with a group, or alongside your son, each day is designed to guide you deeper in character, conviction, and Christlikeness.

This book is divided into five key sections—each one highlighting a vital area of a man's life:

- **A Man's Heart** – identity, integrity, humility, and inner strength

- **A Man's Home** – spiritual leadership, fatherhood, marriage, and family culture

- **A Man's Habits** – discipline, time, money, service, and stewardship

- **A Man's Honor** – speech, friendship, correction, and respect

- **A Man's Holiness** – purity, surrender, obedience, and finishing well

These are not random topics. Together, they form a portrait of the strong, godly man your family, church, and culture truly need.

Each Day's Devotion Includes:

1. Title & Anchor Verse

Each devotional begins with a clear, direct title and a King James Version Scripture verse that grounds the topic in God's Word.

2. Biblical Insight

This short teaching section unpacks the theme for the day with clarity, truth, and pastoral guidance. It's not meant to impress you, but to shape you—to challenge, encourage, and call you to grow.

3. Real-Life Application

Here you'll find 3–5 practical steps you can take to live out that day's truth. These are small, doable actions that build habits over time.

4. This Week's Brick

When it comes to building your home, a strong home, you need bricks. This section provides you with a brick to place each week, each day, each hour, and each moment in the strong wall around your home and the hearts of your children.

This is your focus action—a single, tangible "brick" to lay as you build a life of godliness. It might be a conversation, a decision, or a shift in your thinking. These bricks matter. They add up.

5. Give Yourself Grace

No man is perfect. This section reminds you that the strength we need is not our own. It's a space to breathe, remember the gospel, and receive God's mercy as you grow.

6. Reflection Questions

Use these to pause, journal, or start a conversation with another man. They will help you think deeply and apply truth personally.

7. Prayer

Each day ends with a short, heartfelt prayer. Use it to realign your heart with God and ask for His help as you lead and grow.

Daily Rhythm, Eternal Results

Read one devotion a day. Sit with it. Don't rush. Some days you'll feel convicted. On other days, you'll feel encouraged. That's how God works—shaping you from the inside out.

If you miss a day, come back. If you fall short, return to grace. If you finish strong, pass it on to another man.

You are not walking alone. God is with you. And the men we need are not perfect—but they are present, faithful, and grounded in Christ.

If you're struggling, text me at 704-974-6108. I will pray with you.

WHAT DOES IT MEAN TO BE A STRONG MAN?

We often hear the word 'strong' used to describe all sorts of men—athletes, leaders, fighters, soldiers, and survivors. But biblical strength is not found in the gym, in the paycheck, or in the titles a man earns. It's not measured in how loud he talks or how many people follow him.

Biblical strength begins in the heart—and it starts with surrender.

The Strong Man Is Not Self-Made

Our world celebrates self-made men. But the kingdom of God is built by *God-made* men. Strong men are not perfect. They're not fearless. They're not proud.

Strong men are faithful.

They stand when others run. They bow when others boast. They repent when others justify. They speak truth when it's costly. They stay steady when life shakes.

"Watch ye, stand fast in the faith, quit you like men, be strong."

—1 Corinthians 16:13

The Bible commands men to stand strong—but not in their flesh. Their strength comes from God, and it is shaped by Scripture.

The Strong Man Is Surrendered to Christ

Ephesians 6:10 says, "Be strong in the Lord, and in the power of his might." That is the kind of strength this book calls you to.

Not the strength to dominate, but to serve.

Not the strength to impress, but to obey.

Not the strength to stand alone, but to walk humbly with God.

The Strong Man Shapes His Heart, Home, Habits, Honor, and Holiness

This devotional is divided into five sections that reflect the core areas of a man's life:

• **A Man's Heart** – Identity, humility, repentance, and inner strength

• **A Man's Home** – Marriage, fatherhood, presence, and leadership

• **A Man's Habits** – Discipline, time, money, and consistency

• **A Man's Honor** – Speech, forgiveness, correction, and brotherhood

• **A Man's Holiness** – Purity, surrender, obedience, and finishing well

No man can master all of these in a month. But every man can take one step today—and keep going tomorrow.

The Strong Man Is a Builder

You're not just leading today. You're building something that will outlast you. Your son will carry your voice in his mind. Your daughter will measure other men by your character. Your home will reflect your patterns of faith or neglect.

Strong men leave a trail behind them—and what they build becomes a blessing or a burden to the next generation.

The Strong Man Leans on Grace

You will fall short. We all do. But the strong man knows how to get back up. Not in his own strength, but by God's mercy.

That's why every day in this book includes a moment of grace. You're not on a performance track. You're walking with Christ.

A Personal Word

This book is not just for men with perfect pasts or clean stories. It's for men who want to grow. Men who want to love better. Lead better. Finish better. Men who want to become the kind of man that their wife can trust, their children can follow, and their church can rely on.

We need strong men.

Not just in the pulpit or in the spotlight—but in living rooms, job sites, kitchens, classrooms, and front porches.

That man can be you. Not because you're capable, but because Christ is faithful.

Let's build together.

—John

WHAT IS BIBLICAL MASCULINITY?

Biblical Masculinity Defined

Biblical masculinity is a man's God-given calling to courageously lead, humbly serve, responsibly protect, and faithfully provide—guided by the Word of God, empowered by the Spirit of God, and patterned after the Son of God—for the glory of God and the good of others.

Key Biblical Components

1. Created Male by God's Design

"So God created man in his own image, in the image of God created he him; male and female created he them."

—Genesis 1:27

Masculinity is not a social construct—it is part of God's good creation. Men and women are equal in worth but distinct in role and design. Biblical masculinity embraces this God-ordained distinction with gratitude and reverence.

2. Assigned Responsibility Before Marriage

"And the Lord God took the man, and put him into the garden of Eden to dress it and to keep it."

—Genesis 2:15

Before Adam had a wife or children, he had responsibility. A man who walks in biblical masculinity doesn't wait to be told what to do—he takes initiative under God's authority.

3. Leads with Humility and Strength

"Husbands, love your wives, even as Christ also loved the church, and gave himself for it."

—Ephesians 5:25

Biblical leadership is not domination—it is self-sacrifice. A strong man lays down his life, not his temper. He leads by example, disciplines with grace, and humbles himself before the Lord.

4. Protects and Provides

"But if any provide not for his own, and specially for those of his own house, he hath denied the faith, and is worse than an infidel."

—1 Timothy 5:8

"Quit you like men, be strong."

—1 Corinthians 16:13

Protection is more than physical—it is spiritual and emotional. A biblical man guards his family from compromise, error, and harm. He provides more than a paycheck; he provides presence, direction, and truth.

5. Pursues Holiness and Legacy

"That the man of God may be perfect, throughly furnished unto all good works."

—2 Timothy 3:17

A biblical man fights sin, walks in purity, and finishes well. He understands that his habits today become his children's heritage tomorrow. He is not content to coast—he builds.

Summary

Biblical masculinity is not measured by control, aggression, wealth, or independence. It is measured by Christlikeness.

A biblical man submits to God, lives with conviction, and serves those entrusted to him with love and strength.

A LETTER TO FATHERS RAISING DAUGHTERS

From a grandfather, a father, and a fellow man under God

Dear Dad,

If you're raising a daughter, you are standing at the intersection of heaven's design and a world determined to unravel it.

Your role is irreplaceable.

Your daughter is watching. Not just when you're smiling in the photo, but when you're weighed down and don't realize she notices. She's paying attention to your words—but also your silences. She is learning what strength looks like, what love feels like, and what a godly man lives like… by watching you.

I know this, not only as a minister, but as a father and now a grandfather. My granddaughter Sydney is a precious gift. Her father, John, is raising her with intention and love. And I—her grandfather—am praying and standing alongside them both to ensure Sydney grows up surrounded by men who walk with God and show her what biblical masculinity really means.

The world will offer her loud voices—none of which will sound like truth. The world will define success in terms of performance, identity by feelings, and love by compromise. But God's Word offers a different vision. And you, Dad, are His chosen messenger to deliver it.

You Are Her First Definition of Love

Before she ever hears a sermon about God's love, she will experience it—or question it—through you.

Do you hug her? Speak gently to her? Apologize when you're wrong? Stand firm when she's confused? Your consistency becomes her safety. Your kindness builds her confidence. Your boundaries tell her she's valuable. And your example lays the groundwork for how she will measure every man that comes after.

If she sees respect in your eyes when you speak to her mother, she will know what respect looks like. If she sees tenderness in your hands when you serve, she will expect tenderness from others. If she sees courage in your convictions, she will know that strength and compassion are not enemies.

You Are Her Example of the Father Heart of God

Psalm 144:12 speaks of daughters as "corner stones, polished after the similitude of a palace." That is no small calling. She is meant to be strong, beautiful in character, refined in her spirit, and unshaken by the chaos around her. You help form that.

Let her hear you pray—not just in public, but behind closed doors. Let her see you forgive—not just others, but yourself. Let her know that you fight your battles in the Spirit, and that your strength comes from God, not pride.

Deuteronomy 6 commands us to teach our children diligently. But more than words, they need witnesses. Show her what obedience looks like. Show her what godly sorrow feels like. Show her what joy in Christ really is. That is discipleship.

You Are Her Foundation in a Shaking World

One day, she will walk into places you cannot follow. She'll sit in classrooms, scroll through phones, hear voices—many of them godless and some of them cruel. When the world tries to tell her who she is, may your voice already echo louder:

"You are loved."

"You are seen."

"You are not alone."

"You were made by God, for God, and nothing less will ever satisfy."

Even if she strays, the strength of your investment will call her back. Do not parent for today alone. Parent with eternity in mind.

What Matters Most

Fathers, this matters more than money. More than sports. More than grades. This matters because **your daughter is not just a girl in your home—she is a soul in your care.**

You are not expected to be flawless. But you are expected to be faithful. Walk in the fear of the Lord. Say no to sin. Say yes to the Word. Ask forgiveness when you fail. And lead her, not with the force of dominance, but with the depth of devotion.

You have been entrusted with royalty.

Don't let the noise of this culture drown out the call of heaven: **She needs a strong man—anchored in Christ, guided by truth, filled with grace.**

Let her grow up knowing what godly manhood looks like—because she lived with it.

Sincerely,

John

Father, Grandfather, and Fellow Soldier in the Battle for the Next Generation

A LETTER TO FATHERS RAISING SONS

From one man to another: your legacy is walking beside you

Dear Dad,

If you're raising a son, then you're not just shaping a boy—you're sculpting a man.

And not just any man. You are shaping the man your son will one day become when no one is watching. You are building the man who will lead a home, love a woman, raise children, walk with God, fight sin, and carry your family name into a future you may never see.

That is no small calling.

Every man is a mirror of the men who raised or failed him. If your own father modeled strength, humility, and righteousness, then you've inherited a path worth walking. But if your father fell short—if you carry wounds or silence or confusion from the past—then you have a holy opportunity. You can break the pattern. You can start something new.

Because sons don't just listen to lectures. They live by example.

What Your Son Learns Without You Realizing

He is watching you, even when he pretends he's not. He's watching how you respond to pressure. How you treat his mother. How you handle money. How you laugh. How you pray. How you fall—and how you get back up.

He will imitate your tone. He will adopt your habits. He will either repeat your sins or remember your repentance.

That's why Deuteronomy 6 commands us to impress God's truth on our children—not once, but repeatedly, naturally, and intentionally: when you sit, when you walk, when you rise, when you lie down. The shaping of a man begins long before he holds a Bible or leads a meeting. It begins with how he watches you live your ordinary days.

He Needs Strength—But Not the World's Version

The world says strength is loud. Aggressive. Stoic. Competitive.

But biblical strength is different. It is Spirit-filled. It is self-controlled. It is meekness under pressure. It's Jesus in the garden saying, "Not my will, but thine."

Your son doesn't need to be the toughest in the room. He needs to be the man who stands when it matters, apologizes when he's wrong, and refuses to compromise when the crowd caves in.

Teach him that strength is guarding his eyes, bending his knee, owning his mistakes, carrying others' burdens, and standing on the Word of God when no one else will.

He Will Learn from Your Wins—and Your Wounds

Don't hide your scars. Show him what grace looks like in real time.

Tell him how Christ saved you. Show him how you deal with sin. Let him see what it means to confess, to forgive, to grow.

He doesn't need a flawless father. He needs a real one.

David told Solomon, "Be thou strong therefore, and shew thyself a man" (1 Kings 2:2). That wasn't a pep talk—it was a charge. A father urging his son to rise, to walk with God, and to build a legacy. You can give that same gift.

You Are His Map for Mental, Emotional, Spiritual, and Financial Health

- Mentally—he will believe about himself what you first believed about him.
- Emotionally—he will carry your tone with him. He will know how to love or hold back based on your actions.
- Spiritually—he will either run to God or hide from Him based on how you speak of truth, holiness, and mercy.
- Financially—he will carry your principles. What you praise, spend, avoid, or sacrifice will shape his own stewardship.

You are his first and most formative mentor in every area of life. One day, he will live out your convictions—or your confusion. Choose what you hand him carefully.

One Day, He'll Lead Because You Did

There will be a moment when your son is alone in the world—making a decision that matters. And in that moment, you won't be there to speak. But your voice will echo anyway.

So please give him a faith that's alive. A vision that's biblical. A fatherhood that's intentional. Don't waste this season.

Your son doesn't need a coach. He doesn't need a buddy. He doesn't need a drill sergeant.

He needs a man of God.

Let him learn to pray by hearing you. Let him learn to lead by watching you. Let him learn to stand by walking behind you.

And when he grows into the man God called him to be—he will know who helped him get there.

With you in the fight,

John

Father, Grandfather, and Builder of Men Who Build

PART ONE
A MAN'S HEART

CHAPTER 1
THE WORD IS ENOUGH

Sᴄʀɪᴘᴛᴜʀᴇ:

"Man shall not live by bread alone, but by every word that proceedeth out of the mouth of God." — Deuteronomy 8:3

Biblical Insight:

A man can live without bread longer than he can live without the Word. In Deuteronomy 8:3, God reminds Israel that their survival in the wilderness was not sustained by food alone, but by obedience to every word that came from His mouth. God was training them to depend completely on Him.

As a man, you are constantly tempted to live by effort, accomplishment, and provision. But if the Word is not your foundation, your strength will eventually fail. Spiritual nourishment must come first—not last.

You are only as strong as your dependence on God. Without His voice shaping your inner life, you will drift into self-reliance and spiritual emptiness.

Whether you're raising sons, daughters, or both, your children need to see you living from your God-given identity.

Application:

• Start your day with God's Word, even if only for five minutes.

• Post one verse somewhere visible at home or work this week.

• Let Scripture guide one decision you make today.

Reflection Questions:

• Am I feeding my mind more with media than with Scripture?

• What does my schedule say about the importance of God's Word in my life?

• How has God spoken to me recently through His Word?

This Week's Brick:

Choose one passage of Scripture this week to read, reflect on, and live out. Write it where you will see it every day.

Give Yourself Grace:

If you've been chasing strength in every place but God's Word, stop and return. The Word is still enough. It is alive. It is for you. You can begin again—right now.

Prayer:

Lord,

I confess that I often try to live by my strength and knowledge. But I need Your Word more than my own wisdom. Help me to hunger for Your truth. Let Your Word shape how I think, speak, and lead. Teach me that life is not sustained by what I produce—but by what You have spoken. In Jesus' name, Amen.

CHAPTER 2
LORD, SEARCH ME

SCRIPTURE:

"I the Lord search the heart, I try the reins, even to give every man according to his ways, and according to the fruit of his doings." — Jeremiah 17:10

Biblical Insight:

God is not impressed by outward performance—He inspects the inner man. Jeremiah 17 reminds us that the heart is deceitful and desperately wicked, and that only God truly knows what lies beneath the surface.

Men must search their hearts daily. A godly man does not trust his instincts—he trusts God to reveal what must be confessed, surrendered, and changed.

Heart inventory is essential. God weighs motives, thoughts, desires, and secret sins. He sees what we hide. But His gaze is not one of condemnation—it is one of compassion. When we allow God to search us, we give Him room to cleanse us, restore us, and use us.

Application:

• Set aside time this week to ask God: "What's in my heart that displeases You?"

• Write down what He reveals—repent, and pray for change.

• Begin each morning with Psalm 139:23–24 on your lips: *"Search me, O God…"*

Reflection Questions:

• When was the last time I asked God to search my motives?

• Am I hiding anything in my heart that needs to be exposed and surrendered?

• What part of my character needs refining?

This Week's Brick:

Pray Psalm 139:23–24 aloud each morning this week. Ask God to show you what needs changing—and be still enough to listen.

Give Yourself Grace:

God doesn't reveal your flaws to shame you. He shows you what needs to change because He loves you. Conviction is not rejection—it's invitation.

Prayer:

Father,

I ask You to search me—honestly and thoroughly. Reveal what I've ignored. Uncover what I've excused. Show me where pride, fear, lust, anger, or unbelief still live. I don't want to fake righteousness—I want to walk in truth. Cleanse my heart. Refine my motives. Let me walk uprightly, inside and out. In Jesus' name, Amen.

CHAPTER 3
LEAD ME TO REPENTANCE

SCRIPTURE:

"Or despisest thou the riches of his goodness and forbearance and longsuffering; not knowing that the goodness of God leadeth thee to repentance?" — Romans 2:4

Biblical Insight:

Repentance is not a one-time act—it is a daily response to God's goodness. Romans 2:4 reminds us that God's kindness, not His anger, draws us to repentance. A godly man does not run from conviction; he runs toward grace.

The spiritual man regularly confesses and forsakes sin. He welcomes correction. He refuses to justify his failures or blame others. His strength lies in his willingness to turn back to God quickly.

True manhood is not marked by defiance—it is marked by humility. Repentance is strength under submission. It is what keeps your heart soft, your conscience clear, and your walk close with God.

Application:

•Reflect on one area where God has patiently dealt with you.

•Thank Him for His mercy. Then repent with sincerity and specificity.

•Keep short accounts. Make daily confession a normal part of your time with God.

Reflection Questions:

•What has God been convicting me of recently?

•Have I responded to His conviction with excuses or repentance?

•What keeps me from repenting quickly and freely?

This Week's Brick:

Identify one area of unconfessed sin and take it to God in prayer. If needed, confess it to a trusted brother and receive accountability.

Give Yourself Grace:

God is not surprised by your sin. What grieves Him is when you stay hidden. His kindness is leading you to repentance, not His wrath. Run to Him, not from Him.

Prayer:

Father,

Thank You for Your patience with me. You could have judged me—but You waited. You could have walked away—but You invited me back. I do not want to take Your grace for granted. So today, I turn from what displeases You. Cleanse me. Restore me. Lead me to walk in truth. Teach me to repent as a lifestyle, not just an event. In Jesus' name, Amen.

CHAPTER 4
GUARD YOUR HEART

SCRIPTURE:

"Keep thy heart with all diligence; for out of it are the issues of life." —
Proverbs 4:23

Biblical Insight:

The heart is the control center of your life. Proverbs 4:23 commands
you to guard it—not casually, but *with all diligence*. Why? Because
everything flows from it—your thoughts, choices, words, relationships, and worship.

A wise man does not live on autopilot. He monitors the affections,
temptations, and pressures that try to invade his heart. He knows the
danger of neglect.

Your heart is always under spiritual attack—from pride, lust, bitterness, distractions, or worldly thinking. Satan wants to poison your source so he can pollute your whole life. A godly man stands guard with prayer, Scripture, and accountability.

You cannot delegate this responsibility. No one can guard your heart for you. You must be alert and armed.

Application:

•Identify one thing this week that is trying to pull your heart away from God.

•Set a boundary. Cut off access. Bring it into the light.

•Re-center your heart daily with Scripture and time in prayer.

•Your daughters need to see biblical masculinity just as much as your sons need to follow it. Your leadership and love shape how they view strength and grace.

Reflection Questions:

•What influences are shaping my heart right now—for better or worse?

•Have I allowed entertainment, bitterness, or distraction to take root?

•What one boundary do I need to put in place this week?

This Week's Brick:

This week, identify one source that pollutes your heart—media, music, bitterness, distraction—and create a boundary to protect your mind and spirit.

Give Yourself Grace:

If your heart has been unguarded, God's mercy still flows. The damage isn't final. He can restore what was exposed. Start fresh. Lock the gate.

Prayer:

Lord,

Help 'me guard my heart. Show me what does not belong—jealousy, pride, impurity, fear, or anger. I want to be diligent, not passive. Keep me from slowly drifting. Help me stay alert, grounded in Your Word, and accountable to Your Spirit. May my heart stay pure, because I want my life to honor You. In Jesus' name, Amen.

CHAPTER 5
A HUMBLE MAN IS A STRONG MAN

SCRIPTURE:

"God resisteth the proud, but giveth grace unto the humble." — James 4:6

Biblical Insight:

In God's kingdom, humility is power. James 4:6 draws a sharp line: pride brings resistance from God; humility invites His grace. A godly man doesn't inflate his image—he bows his heart.

Men must live examined lives, not defensive ones. Pride resists correction. Pride refuses confession. Pride rejects dependence on others. But humility unlocks every door the proud man slams shut.

A humble man listens. He learns. He serves. He admits when he is wrong. His strength is not in control—but in surrender. And that surrender gives him influence. Pride tries to lead through fear; humility leads through faith.

God does not bless the proud father, the proud husband, the proud servant. He gives grace to the man who knows he needs it.

Application:

• Confess one area where pride has kept you from asking for help.

• Apologize this week to someone you've wronged or ignored.

• Begin your prayers with these words: *"Lord, I need You."*

Reflection Questions:

• Where is pride showing up in my words, habits, or relationships?

• Have I confused stubbornness with strength?

• How would my home change if I walked more humbly?

This Week's Brick:

Ask someone close to you this week: "Where do I need to grow?" Receive their answer with humility—not defense. Then pray through what they said.

Give Yourself Grace:

Humility is not weakness. Admitting your need is strength in God's eyes. Even if you've been proud or resistant, His grace is still yours.

Prayer:

Father,

I need Your grace more than I need control. Forgive my pride—my desire to always be right, always be strong, always be admired. Break that in me. Teach me that humility is not weakness—it is strength under surrender. Clothe me in lowliness of heart. Make me a man who kneels before You and lifts others up. In Jesus' name, Amen.

CHAPTER 6
A MAN AFTER GOD'S OWN HEART

SCRIPTURE:

"And when he had removed him, he raised up unto them David to be their king; to whom also he gave testimony, and said, I have found David the son of Jesse, a man after mine own heart, which shall fulfil all my will." — Acts 13:22

Biblical Insight:

God is not looking for the strongest, smartest, or most skilled. He is looking for men whose hearts chase His.

David was not perfect. He sinned grievously. Yet God said David was "a man after mine own heart." Why? Because David was quick to repent, eager to obey, and sincere in his pursuit of God.

Every man must take daily heart inventory. The question is not: "Am I impressive?" but "Am I surrendered?" A man after God's heart lives for the audience of One. He cares more about pleasing God than about appearing righteous.

David fulfilled God's will not because of flawless performance, but because of faithful pursuit. He made room for correction. He loved God's Word. He lived in honesty before God. And when he fell, he returned—not ran.

Application:

•Spend time in Psalm 51 this week—David's prayer of repentance. Make it your own.

•Ask God to realign your heart with His.

•Make one decision today based not on what you want, but what God wants.

Reflection Questions:

•What keeps me from fully chasing after God's heart?

•When did I last ask God to reshape my desires to match His?

•Am I more concerned with reputation or with obedience?

This Week's Brick:

Ask God this week to reshape your desires. Write down one thing you love that draws you closer to Him—and one that pulls you away. Pursue one. Lay down the other.

Give Yourself Grace:

You don't have to be flawless to be faithful. God called David a man after His own heart, even after failure. What matters most is your direction—not just your history.

Prayer:

Lord,

Make me a man after Your heart. I do not want to live for approval, applause, or control. I want to fulfill Your will. Cleanse my motives. Sharpen my conscience. Lead my heart to worship, to serve, to obey. When I fall, help me run back to You. Let my life reflect a heart that beats in rhythm with Yours. In Jesus' name, Amen.

PART TWO
A MAN'S HOME

CHAPTER 7
LEADING YOUR FAMILY SPIRITUALLY

Scripture:

"And thou shalt teach them diligently unto thy children, and shalt talk of them when thou sittest in thine house, and when thou walkest by the way, and when thou liest down, and when thou risest up." — Deuteronomy 6:7

Biblical Insight:

God didn't assign spiritual leadership to the pastor, youth director, or Sunday School teacher. He gave it to fathers.

In Deuteronomy 6, right after commanding Israel to love God wholeheartedly, He called fathers to teach their children diligently. The home was—and still is—God's chosen classroom. Spiritual leadership is not about being the loudest, most educated, or most charismatic. It is about being present, intentional, and faithful.

Men, our leadership begins at home. A man may lead in public, but if he neglects to lead spiritually in his home, he forfeits his credibility.

You do not have to know everything to teach your children. You simply have to love God and open His Word. Speak of truth when you sit, walk, lie down, and rise up. Your home becomes a sanctuary—not because of candles or quiet—but because Scripture and prayer dwell there.

Whether you're raising sons, daughters, or both, your example of provision speaks volumes about who God is.

Application:

• Open the Bible at the dinner table once this week. Read one verse aloud.

• Ask your children, "What's one thing I can pray for you about today?"

• Make Sunday worship a non-negotiable rhythm in your family.

Reflection Questions:

• Am I actively teaching my children about the Lord, or passively hoping they learn it elsewhere?

• What spiritual habits can I start or strengthen in our home?

• How can I lead by example, not just words?

This Week's Brick:

Lead a short time of prayer or Scripture reading with your family at least once this week. Keep it simple and sincere.

Give Yourself Grace:

If you've avoided this role out of fear, guilt, or uncertainty, know this: you're not too late. Start with what you have. God will meet you as you lead—even imperfectly.

Prayer:

Father,

You gave me this home, this family, and this responsibility. Help me lead spiritually—not out of fear, but by faith. Let my example be consistent, my words full of truth, and my habits worthy of imitation. When I feel inadequate, remind me that You equip those You call. Make my house a place where Your name is spoken, honored, and lived. In Jesus' name, Amen.

CHAPTER 8
LOVE YOUR WIFE LIKE
CHRIST LOVED THE CHURCH

SCRIPTURE:

"Husbands, love your wives, even as Christ also loved the church, and gave himself for it." — Ephesians 5:25

Biblical Insight:

Your children are learning how to love—by watching how you love their mother.

Ephesians 5:25 doesn't command a man to simply "stay married" or "provide financially." It calls him to love like Christ. That means sacrifice, patience, grace, service, and the willingness to lay down self.

A man must be a **Leader, Lover, and Learner** in his marriage. To love your wife is to lead her gently, to serve her joyfully, and to study her intentionally. This kind of love is not driven by feelings but by commitment.

When a father loves his wife like Christ loved the church, it creates security in the home. It models the gospel. It teaches your sons what to become and your daughters what to expect.

You are not just loving your wife—you are shaping your family's future by doing so.

Application:

•Do one sacrificial act of love for your wife this week—unasked, unexpected, and intentional.

•Speak a word of praise about her in front of your children.

•Ask her, "What's one way I can better show you love this week?"

Reflection Questions:

•Would my wife say she feels cherished, not just provided for?

•What attitudes or habits have crept into my heart that diminish my love for her?

•How does my love for my wife reflect Christ's love for me?

This Week's Brick:

Do one intentional act of love for your wife this week—without expecting anything in return. Serve her in a way that reflects Christ's selflessness.

Give Yourself Grace:

If your love has been inconsistent, selfish, or strained, Christ's love never fails. You are loved. You can love again. Grace isn't just for receiving—it's for giving.

Prayer:

Lord Jesus,

You loved me when I was unlovable. You gave everything to rescue and redeem. Help me to love my wife with that same humility and grace. Teach me to serve, not to demand. Show me how to cherish her in word and deed. Where I've grown cold or selfish, warm my heart again. Let my love be a reflection of the gospel. In Jesus' name, Amen.

CHAPTER 9
THE MINISTRY OF PRESENCE

SCRIPTURE:

"Lo, children are an heritage of the Lord: and the fruit of the womb is his reward." — Psalm 127:3

Biblical Insight:

You do not need to be perfect to be a good father—you need to be present.

Psalm 127:3 reminds us that children are not burdens to manage but blessings to steward. They are God's reward to you, not a distraction from your real work. Your presence in their lives—consistent, calm, engaged—is ministry. When you show up, you tell your children, "You matter."

A godly man orders his life by biblical priorities. A man's spiritual leadership starts by being available. Your work ethic provides for your family, but your physical and emotional presence anchors them.

You do not have to plan extravagant outings or deliver eloquent devotions every night. But when your children see your face, hear your voice, and know you are near, their hearts are strengthened.

Presence gives your words weight. It builds trust. It turns moments into memories.

Application:

•Set your phone aside during key parts of the day: meals, bedtime, and conversations.

•Schedule one "Dad Time" moment this week: a walk, game, or conversation—just the two of you.

•Ask your children, "How can I spend better time with you?"

Reflection Questions:

•Am I physically present but emotionally absent in my home?

•What simple habit could help me show up more intentionally each day?

•How does my view of time reflect my value for my children?

This Week's Brick:

Choose one setting this week—mealtime, bedtime, or a car ride—to put down your phone, close the laptop, and be fully present with your family.

Give Yourself Grace:

You're pulled in a hundred directions. But presence is more powerful than perfection. Even if you've missed moments before, God can redeem today.

Prayer:

Father,

Thank You for the gift of my children. Help me not to miss their hearts while chasing the world. Let me show up, not just check in. Teach me to listen, to enjoy, to linger in their world. When I'm tired, remind me that presence is worship. Help me to treasure the time You've given and to invest it well. In Jesus' name, Amen.

CHAPTER 10
DISCIPLINE WITH GRACE

SCRIPTURE:

"He that spareth his rod hateth his son: but he that loveth him chasteneth him betimes." — Proverbs 13:24

Biblical Insight:

Discipline is an act of love, not an outlet for anger. Proverbs 13:24 challenges fathers to see correction as proof of affection. A father who refuses to discipline is not being gentle—he's being negligent.

God disciplines His children because He loves them (Hebrews 12:6). In the same way, a father reflects God's character when he lovingly corrects his child to shape their heart, not just stop their behavior.

A father must lead with intentionality, not reaction. Discipline must never be impulsive, abusive, or shaming. It should be timely, clear, and always followed by restoration.

Children learn not just from what we discipline—but from how. The tone, timing, and truth behind the correction are what linger in their hearts. When grace and truth are combined, discipline becomes a doorway to wisdom.

Application:

•Discipline your child only after prayer—ask God for wisdom and calm.

•After correcting your child, affirm your love and explain why you corrected them.

•Evaluate your methods: Are they firm but fair? Biblical but gracious?

Reflection Questions:

•Do I discipline to restore or just to control?

•What is my tone like when I correct my children?

•Am I consistent, or do I discipline based on my mood?

This Week's Brick:

Before disciplining your child this week, pause to pray—"Lord, help me reflect You." Then speak correction with truth and love.

Give Yourself Grace:

If you've disciplined from frustration instead of love, confess and reset. God disciplines us with mercy. So can you. Your failure is not final.**Prayer:**

Father,

Thank You for correcting me in love and not in wrath. Help me reflect that same heart when I discipline my children. Teach me to be patient, not reactive. Help me guide, not just punish. Give me wisdom to shape their hearts, not just their habits. Let my discipline build trust, not fear. In Jesus' name, Amen.

CHAPTER 11
BUILD A GOD-HONORING FAMILY CULTURE

SCRIPTURE:

"And if it seem evil unto you to serve the Lord, choose you this day whom ye will serve... but as for me and my house, we will serve the Lord." — Joshua 24:15

Biblical Insight:

Every home has a culture. It may be loud or quiet, structured or spontaneous, peaceful or tense—but it exists. And that culture is not formed by accident. It is shaped by leadership. Joshua made a bold declaration: *"As for me and my house, we will serve the Lord."*

A godly man doesn't merely lead family devotions—he leads a family direction. His choices set the rhythm of the home. His words set the tone. His habits create an atmosphere where God's presence is welcome.

Leadership in the home must be intentional. Men are to set the climate of spiritual warmth, relational connection, and gospel-centered values.

Your home should feel different—not because it's perfect, but because it's centered on God's Word and grace. That's what it means to build a culture that honors the Lord.

Application:

•Declare together as a family: *"We will serve the Lord."* Post it somewhere visible.

•Choose one family rhythm this week—prayer at the table, reading Scripture together, or singing a hymn.

•Talk with your spouse or children about what kind of home you want to build.

Reflection Questions:

•What is the spiritual atmosphere of my home?

•What habits need to be removed or introduced to honor God more fully?

•Would someone visiting our home sense that we serve the Lord?

This Week's Brick:

Have a family conversation this week about what your home values most. Choose one small habit to reflect those values—like praying before meals or blessing one another with words.

Give Yourself Grace:

If your home has drifted or lacked direction, you're not stuck. One decision made in humility can change your family's future. Culture doesn't happen overnight—but it starts with you.

Prayer:

Lord,

Help me build a home that honors You. Let Your Word shape our choices, Your presence fill our space, and Your truth guide our conversations. Give me wisdom to lead with clarity and humility. Make our home a place where peace, grace, and worship live. May my house serve You—not just in words, but in every decision we make. In Jesus' name, Amen.

.

PART THREE
A MAN'S HABITS

CHAPTER 12
THE POWER OF DAILY DISCIPLINE

SCRIPTURE:

"He that is faithful in that which is least is faithful also in much…" — Luke 16:10a

Biblical Insight:

God is not measuring your greatness by what you accomplish in a year, but by what you steward in a day. Luke 16:10 teaches that faithfulness in small things proves readiness for greater responsibility.

Spiritual maturity is not built in dramatic moments—it's formed in daily disciplines. Reading Scripture, praying, managing your time, finishing what you start—these are the bricks of a godly life.

The Christian life must be marked by structure, purpose, and submission. Habits are how a man lives out his values. Good intentions do not replace faithful action.

Discipline does not enslave you—it frees you. It keeps you consistent when motivation fades. It helps you become a man others can trust and a vessel God can use.

Whether you're raising sons, daughters, or both, each child needs a clear and personal picture of who Jesus is—through you.

Application:

•Choose one new spiritual habit this week: prayer at a set time, Bible reading, or journaling.

•Set a time and place where this habit will live.

•Track your progress, and don't quit if you miss a day—restart the next.

Reflection Questions:

•What daily habits are shaping who I'm becoming?

•Where am I excusing inconsistency rather than correcting it?

•What one habit, if practiced faithfully, would grow my walk with God?

This Week's Brick:

Choose one daily habit this week to pursue with consistency—Bible reading, prayer, or even a physical discipline—and ask God to help you follow through.

Give Yourself Grace:

Discipline isn't perfection—it's practice. If you've struggled to stick with routines, don't quit. God honors every small step. Keep showing up. He is faithful in the process.

Prayer:

Father,

Teach me to be faithful in the little things. Help me honor You in the quiet moments, the small decisions, and the unseen routines. Form in me the character of Christ through daily discipline. Strengthen my will to match Your Word. Let my life reflect steady obedience, not just occasional inspiration. In Jesus' name, Amen.

CHAPTER 13
STEWARDING TIME WISELY

Scripture:

"See then that ye walk circumspectly, not as fools, but as wise, redeeming the time, because the days are evil." — Ephesians 5:15–16

Biblical Insight:

Time is a gift you cannot save, pause, or relive. Ephesians 5 urges believers to walk carefully and wisely—redeeming the time—because the world is dark, and opportunities are fleeting.

A foolish man drifts through life with little thought of how he uses his hours. A wise man redeems time—he buys it back, uses it for what matters, and shapes it for eternity.

Men must live with a spiritual margin. A crowded life often reveals a disordered heart. What fills your calendar reveals what drives your priorities.

Stewarding time wisely is not about packing your day—it's about aligning your time with God's purpose. It's about saying "yes" to the eternal and "no" to the trivial.

Application:

• Audit your last 24 hours. What did you do that mattered most?

• Identify one time-waster and replace it with a God-honoring rhythm.

• Plan tomorrow before it begins. Build margin for people, prayer, and reflection.

Reflection Questions:

• What do my routines say about my priorities?

• Am I constantly rushed or intentionally ordered?

• What one small change could create more space for what matters most?

This Week's Brick:

Track how you spend your time over the next three days. Identify one area of waste—and one place where time with God or family can be prioritized.

Give Yourself Grace:

You can't get back wasted time—but God can redeem the time ahead. Don't let regret stop you. Stewardship starts with awareness, and it grows through grace.

Prayer:

Lord,

You gave me today as a gift. Help me use it wisely. Teach me to number my days. Show me what to cut and what to keep. Help me reject distraction and embrace purpose. May I live this day with eternity in view. Let my time be redeemed for Your glory. In Jesus' name, Amen.

CHAPTER 14
GIVE, SAVE, SPEND – HONORING GOD WITH YOUR FINANCES

SCRIPTURE:

"Honour the Lord with thy substance, and with the firstfruits of all thine increase." — Proverbs 3:9

Biblical Insight:

Money reveals your values. Where you give, how you save, and what you spend reflect what matters most to you. Proverbs 3:9 commands believers to honor God with *everything* they have—not just words or intentions, but wealth and resources.

Biblical stewardship is not about how much you make, but how you manage what you've been given. Christian men must honor God by giving generously, saving wisely, and spending carefully. God owns it all—you are a manager, not an owner.

When a man handles his finances with integrity, discipline, and generosity, he reflects the heart of the Father who provides. Tithing is a starting point, not a ceiling. Saving shows foresight. Contentment guards against covetousness.

Your money is not just financial—it's spiritual. It's not just a budget—it's a testimony.

Application:

•Give first. Honor God with the first portion of every paycheck.

•Save second. Create a savings plan that reflects wisdom and planning.

•Spend last. Budget the rest in alignment with your values and needs.

Reflection Questions:

•Does my financial life show that I trust God—or that I trust myself?

•Am I teaching my children to give, save, and spend with purpose?

•Where have I failed to honor God with my substance—and how can I change?

This Week's Brick:

This week, give a financial gift—small or large—with no strings attached. Let generosity, not guilt, guide your stewardship.

Give Yourself Grace:

If money has been a source of stress, pride, or shame, bring it to God. He sees the heart, not the number. Grace flows even into your finances.

Prayer:

Lord,

Everything I have belongs to You. Help me honor You with my income, my spending, my saving, and my giving. Teach me to be wise, generous, and content. Guard me from greed and selfishness. Help me manage what You've entrusted to me in a way that brings glory to You. In Jesus' name, Amen.

CHAPTER 15
ACCOUNTABILITY IS STRENGTH, NOT WEAKNESS

SCRIPTURE:

"Iron sharpeneth iron; so a man sharpeneth the countenance of his friend." — Proverbs 27:17

Biblical Insight:

You were not made to walk alone. Proverbs 27:17 tells us that godly friendship is like iron sharpening iron—bringing strength, clarity, and edge to a man's life.

Accountability is not about control—it's about growth. It is the habit of inviting another man to ask you the hard questions and tell you the hard truths. Spiritual isolation is dangerous. When a man hides his struggles, pride grows. When he shares them, grace flows.

God uses the honesty of a brother to sharpen our thinking, convict our conscience, and strengthen our walk. You cannot lead well, love well, or live well if you refuse to be known. Accountability gives you guardrails when you drift and a mirror when you forget who you are in Christ.

A man who avoids accountability weakens his witness. A man who embraces it multiplies his strength.

Application:

•Reach out to a trusted brother in Christ and ask for regular check-ins.

•Share one area where you want to grow, and give permission for questions.

•Don't just ask for accountability—be accountable.

Reflection Questions:

•Who really knows the state of my heart and mind?

•What fear or pride is keeping me from inviting accountability?

•How would my integrity grow if I gave someone permission to sharpen me?

This Week's Brick:

Ask one godly man this week to check in with you spiritually. Tell him one area where you need encouragement or correction.

Give Yourself Grace:

You were never meant to carry this alone. Accountability doesn't expose you—it protects you. God gives you brothers for a reason. Let them walk beside you.

Prayer:

Father,

Thank You for the brothers in Christ who walk beside me. Help me to reject isolation and embrace accountability. Give me the humility to be honest and the courage to be sharpened. Let my relationships with other men lead me closer to You—not away. Shape me through the truth spoken in love. In Jesus' name, Amen.

CHAPTER 16
THE HABIT OF SERVICE

SCRIPTURE:

"But he that is greatest among you shall be your servant." — Matthew 23:11

Biblical Insight:

True greatness is not found in position—it is found in serving others. Jesus redefined manhood when He declared that the greatest among us must be a servant.

A man of God is not measured by how many follow him, but by how many he lifts. Spiritual men seek the towel, not the throne. They look for opportunities to bless, not be noticed.

Serving others is not a seasonal act—it must become a daily habit.

Your home, your church, your workplace, and your community should all bear the fingerprints of your service.

When service becomes a habit, humility becomes a way of life.

Application:

•Look for one task this week that feels "beneath you"—and do it with joy.

•Ask your wife, pastor, or friend: "How can I serve you this week?"

•Make service a family rhythm—let your children see you lead through humility.

Reflection Questions:

•Do I serve out of love—or only when asked or rewarded?

•What roles in my home or church need a servant—and can I step in?

•How does my attitude about service reflect my heart for Christ?

This Week's Brick:

Look for a quiet, unrecognized opportunity to serve someone this week—at home, church, or work. Do it without announcing it.

Give Yourself Grace:

You don't need a spotlight to be significant. Service forms you into Christlikeness. Even if no one notices—God sees. And He smiles when His sons serve.

Prayer:

Lord,

Make me a servant. Teach me that greatness is found in humility. Help me to do the unseen things with joy and excellence. Let my home, church, and community feel the impact of a man who lives to bless others. Shape my heart through service. Teach me to walk in the steps of the One who came not to be ministered unto, but to minister. In Jesus' name, Amen.

CHAPTER 17
REST IS NOT LAZINESS

Scripture:

"Six days thou shalt labour, and do all thy work: But the seventh day is the sabbath of the Lord thy God: in it thou shalt not do any work…" — Exodus 20:9–10a

Biblical Insight:

Rest is not a reward for finishing everything—it is a command from the Lord. God set the pattern Himself. He created, then He ceased. He worked with purpose and then paused with intention.

Exodus 20 commands us to rest—not because we are lazy, but because we are limited. Men cannot ignore the biblical rhythm of work and rest. A man who never stops working often ends up hollow, distracted, and spiritually dry.

Rest is an act of faith. It says, "God is in control—I am not. The world will go on if I pause." It allows time for reflection, family, worship, and renewal. Rest is not idleness; it is obedience.

The man who learns to rest well will lead well. He will think clearly, love patiently, and serve joyfully.

Application:

•Choose one day or half-day this week to rest from labor and be present with God and your family.

•Turn off distractions—use the time for worship, prayer, Scripture, or conversation.

•Evaluate your weekly rhythm: where do you need to make room for margin?

Reflection Questions:

•Am I working so hard that I've forgotten to enjoy the life God gave me?

•What fears keep me from resting?

•How would my spiritual health change if I took rest seriously?

This Week's Brick:

Choose one evening this week to rest with intention—turn off your devices, read the Word, spend time with family, and trust that God is working while you rest.

Give Yourself Grace:

Rest is not a reward for finishing your list—it's a gift from God. If you're tired, it's not failure. Jesus rested. So can you.

Prayer:

Father,

You gave me work to fulfill and rest to enjoy. Help me not to confuse busyness with faithfulness. Teach me to trust You enough to pause. Restore my heart through rest. Give me the courage to slow down, the wisdom to prioritize, and the grace to enjoy stillness in Your presence. In Jesus' name, Amen.

PART FOUR
A MAN'S HONOR

CHAPTER 18
SPEAK WITH PURPOSE

SCRIPTURE:

"Let your speech be alway with grace, seasoned with salt, that ye may know how ye ought to answer every man." — Colossians 4:6

Biblical Insight:

Your words build worlds—or burn them down.

Paul instructs believers to let their speech be *always with grace*. Not occasionally. Not selectively. Always. God calls men to speak with clarity, kindness, truth, and purpose.

The tongue reveals the heart. A godly man does not speak carelessly. He understands that his words leave marks—on his wife, children, coworkers, and church family.

Grace-filled speech is not soft; it's sacred. It confronts without crushing. It affirms without flattery. It teaches without shaming.

Your words either open doors to Christ—or close them.

Application:

•Choose one conversation today to slow down and speak with grace.

•Catch and correct one negative pattern: sarcasm, sharpness, or complaining.

•Write or speak one word of encouragement to someone who needs it.

Reflection Questions:

•Are my words marked by grace or by frustration?

•Do my children hear more correction than encouragement?

•What would change if I slowed down and spoke to bless, not just to be heard?

This Week's Brick:

Take note of your words this week. Intentionally speak one blessing to your wife, one encouragement to your child, and one testimony of faith to someone else.

Give Yourself Grace:

If your words have wounded more than they've built up, there is still time to speak life. Your mouth can become a tool of healing—God is patient as He teaches you.

Prayer:

Father,

Help me to speak like Jesus. Let my words reflect Your grace, not my mood. Guard my mouth from anger, sarcasm, or pride. Teach me to use my voice to build, bless, and guide. Let my wife, children, and those around me hear truth wrapped in love. In Jesus' name, Amen.

CHAPTER 19
FORGIVE QUICKLY AND FULLY

SCRIPTURE:

"And be ye kind one to another, tenderhearted, forgiving one another, even as God for Christ's sake hath forgiven you." — Ephesians 4:32

Biblical Insight:

Nothing tests your manhood like forgiveness.

Forgiveness is not weakness—it is obedience. Ephesians 4:32 calls us to forgive just as God forgave us. Not partially. Not conditionally. Not eventually. But fully and immediately.

Honor in relationships begins with humility. Bitterness hardens a man. But forgiveness frees him to lead with grace.

When you refuse to forgive, you carry a weight that poisons your perspective. It affects how you speak, how you trust, how you lead. But when you release the offense, you reflect the heart of Christ.

Your family, friends, and church don't need a man who remembers every wrong—they need a man who knows how to let go.

Application:

•Identify one person you've withheld forgiveness from—and begin praying for them by name.

•Take the first step toward reconciliation, even if it's just an honest conversation.

•Remind yourself: Forgiveness is a choice, not a feeling.

Reflection Questions:

•Who have I silently resented—and how is it affecting my heart?

•Have I made forgiveness harder than God made it for me?

•What would change if I extended the same mercy I've received?

This Week's Brick:

This week, release one offense you've been holding—either in prayer or through a conversation. Don't wait for the apology to obey Christ.

Give Yourself Grace:

Forgiveness may feel costly, but bitterness is more expensive. God has forgiven you fully—so you can forgive freely. Even if it takes time, grace leads the way.

Prayer:

Lord,

Thank You for forgiving me. I don't deserve it, but You gave it freely. Help me forgive like that. Crush my pride, soften my heart, and give me courage to let go. Heal what's broken. Restore what bitterness has robbed. Make me a man who forgives quickly and fully. In Jesus' name, Amen.

CHAPTER 20
BE CORRECTABLE

SCRIPTURE:

"Reprove not a scorner, lest he hate thee: rebuke a wise man, and he will love thee." — Proverbs 9:8

Biblical Insight:

The difference between a fool and a wise man is how they respond to correction.

Proverbs 9:8 teaches that a wise man doesn't resist rebuke—he receives it. In fact, he *loves* the person who sharpens him. Why? Because correction makes him better.

Men must pursue accountability and humility. A man who honors God must also honor the truth—even when it stings. If no one can correct you, you are not leading in strength—you are living in pride.

Being correctable means you welcome growth. You recognize your blind spots. You don't defend your flaws—you deal with them.

Correction is not rejection. It is a gift from God through the people who care enough to speak the truth.

Your daughters need to see that real strength includes confession and restoration—not just for their sake, but for their future faith.

Application:

•Ask someone you trust: "Is there anything I'm doing that I'm not seeing clearly?"

•When corrected, listen without interrupting. Reflect before reacting.

•Thank the person who gave correction—even if it was hard to hear.

Reflection Questions:

•Do I react with humility or defensiveness when corrected?

•What was my last response to a rebuke—and what did it reveal?

•What one area do I need to invite correction in this week?

This Week's Brick:

Invite one person you trust to speak into your life this week. Ask them where you could grow—and listen with humility.

Give Yourself Grace:

Correction doesn't mean condemnation. God corrects those He loves. If receiving truth is hard, ask for grace to welcome it—not as an attack, but as an answer to prayer.

Prayer:

Lord,

Make me teachable. When I'm wrong, help me listen. When I'm blind, help me see. Give me the humility to receive truth and the courage to change. Remove pride from my heart and help me grow through the voices You've placed in my life. In Jesus' name, Amen.

CHAPTER 21
HONOR ALL MEN

SCRIPTURE:

"Honour all men. Love the brotherhood. Fear God. Honour the king." — 1 Peter 2:17

Biblical Insight:

Respect is not reserved for those who earn it—it is commanded for all. Peter's words are simple and strong: *"Honour all men."*

This includes the difficult, the different, the overlooked, the undeserving. Honor is not flattery—it is the recognition that every person bears the image of God.

Biblical manhood includes respect for authority, dignity in relationships, and a Christlike attitude toward others. A man of honor doesn't belittle people, mock leadership, or stir division. He treats others with the same grace he has received.

In a world where contempt is common, biblical men must model something better. When you speak with dignity, serve without bias, and lead with respect, you reflect the heart of Christ.

Application:

•Speak kindly about someone this week who may not "deserve" it.

•Correct someone's name, status, or story if they're being mocked or misrepresented.

•Write a note or message of encouragement to someone often overlooked.

Reflection Questions:

•Do I give honor only to those who agree with me or benefit me?

•What does my speech say about how I view others?

•Who in my life needs to be treated with more visible respect?

This Week's Brick:

This week, intentionally speak or show honor to someone who often gets overlooked—at church, at work, or in your home.

Give Yourself Grace:

If you've been quick to judge or slow to show respect, grace still welcomes you back. Honor isn't earned—it's commanded. And when you give it, God is honored, too.

Prayer:

Father,

You made every person in Your image. Help me honor them—not because they've earned it, but because You've commanded it. Remove arrogance, sarcasm, or pride from my speech. Let my heart be respectful, my tone gracious, and my example Christlike. In Jesus' name, Amen.

CHAPTER 22
BE A FAITHFUL FRIEND

SCRIPTURE:

"A friend loveth at all times, and a brother is born for adversity." — Proverbs 17:17

Biblical Insight:

You don't need a crowd—but you do need a brother.

Proverbs 17:17 says a true friend loves at all times—not just when it's easy, not only when things go well. And when hardship hits, that friend becomes like a brother—loyal, present, and steady.

Biblical manhood requires intentional friendships. Too many men isolate. They hide their struggles, avoid hard conversations, and pretend they're fine. But God created you for community—not independence.

A faithful friend encourages when you're weary, speaks truth when you're wandering, and stays when others walk away. He doesn't just watch your life—he helps carry it.

And you must be that kind of man too.

Application:

• Reach out to a friend today. Ask, "How can I pray for you?"

• Follow through: check in, speak truth, show up.

• Be vulnerable—share something real, not rehearsed.

Reflection Questions:

• Who are the men in my life who truly know me?

• Am I available when my friends face adversity—or only when it's convenient?

• What does my friendship say about my faithfulness?

This Week's Brick:

Reach out to one friend this week—just to check in, pray for them, or ask how they're doing. Don't wait for them to go first.

Give Yourself Grace:

Friendship takes effort. And if you've failed to show up in the past, it's not too late to start now. God is the friend who never leaves—and He is shaping you to reflect Him.

Prayer:

Lord,

Thank You for the friends who have stood by me. Help me be that kind of friend in return. Let my relationships be marked by loyalty, encouragement, and grace. Teach me to show up in hard seasons, speak truth when it's needed, and love without conditions. In Jesus' name, Amen.

PART FIVE
A MAN'S HOLINESS

CHAPTER 23
PURITY IS STILL GOD'S STANDARD

SCRIPTURE:

"Blessed are the pure in heart: for they shall see God." — Matthew 5:8

Biblical Insight:

Purity is not outdated—it's essential. In a world that mocks it, Jesus calls it *blessed*.

Matthew 5:8 connects purity to vision. When a man's heart is pure, he sees God clearly—His truth, His will, His beauty. But when sin clouds your heart, it also blurs your view of Him.

Men are to guard their hearts and eyes. Purity begins long before a decision—it starts with what you love, what you allow, and what you pursue. A man who wants to live holy must not flirt with sin or make peace with compromise.

You do not pursue purity out of fear—but out of faith. You want more than momentary pleasure. You want the joy of walking closely with a holy God.

Application:

•Set a guard on your eyes—monitor what you view and how long you linger.

•Confess any secret sin to God, and if needed, to a trusted brother.

•Memorize Matthew 5:8 and pray it every morning this week.

Reflection Questions:

•What am I feeding my heart and mind throughout the day?

•Have I lowered God's standard of purity to make room for my habits?

•What would it look like to pursue purity in thought, speech, and behavior?

This Week's Brick:

Set a new boundary this week to protect your purity—what you watch, read, scroll, or entertain. Let someone hold you accountable.

Give Yourself Grace:

If purity feels like a losing battle, don't give up. God is patient. His grace doesn't excuse sin, but it empowers holiness. His mercy can cleanse even what you've hidden.

Prayer:

Lord,

I want to see You clearly. Cleanse my heart from sin, compromise, and anything that defiles. Make me a man who longs for purity—not just for reputation, but for fellowship with You. Help me walk in light, not darkness. Strengthen me to say no to temptation and yes to holiness. In Jesus' name, Amen.

CHAPTER 24
GUARD YOUR EYES AND MIND

SCRIPTURE:

"I made a covenant with mine eyes; why then should I think upon a maid?" —
Job 31:1

Biblical Insight:

What enters through your eyes doesn't just pass through—it takes root. Job 31:1 is a declaration of discipline: Job made a covenant, a firm commitment, to guard his eyes so that lust would not rule his thoughts.

In a world filled with visual temptation, godly men must be proactive —not reactive. You cannot coast into holiness. You must decide in advance where to look, when to turn away, and how to renew your mind.

Men must examine what they feed their hearts. That feeding begins with the eyes. What you watch, read, scroll, and linger over shapes your desires.

You can't expect to think clearly if you view carelessly. Holiness begins when you guard the gate.

Application:

• Set up filters or limits on your devices to remove easy temptation.

• Redirect your gaze—when you're tempted, look away and pray.

• Fill your mind with Scripture and truth to rewire what you crave.

Reflection Questions:

• What images or messages have I allowed to shape my thinking?

• Do I have guardrails in place—or am I hoping to never crash?

• Am I more afraid of being caught—or of being distant from God?

This Week's Brick:

Choose one day this week to fast from digital distractions. Replace screen time with Scripture, reflection, or quiet worship.

Give Yourself Grace:

What fills your eyes fills your mind—and God knows how easy it is to get drawn in. Guarding yourself is not about legalism; it's about love. If you've looked in the wrong direction, turn your eyes again.

Prayer:

Father,

My eyes wander easily. Help me guard what I look at and think about. Make me vigilant, not passive. Purify my imagination. Let my mind dwell on what is true, pure, lovely, and right. Make me a man whose thoughts honor You, even when no one sees. In Jesus' name, Amen.

CHAPTER 25
HOLINESS IN PRIVATE AND PUBLIC

SCRIPTURE:

"The integrity of the upright shall guide them: but the perverseness of transgressors shall destroy them." — Proverbs 11:3

Biblical Insight:

Your real character is who you are when no one is looking. Proverbs 11:3 tells us that integrity—not appearances—guides the upright. But a double life will destroy you.

Holiness is not just for the spotlight. It is for the shadows—the quiet moments, the private habits, the hidden decisions. What you tolerate in secret will eventually shape your public witness.

A man must walk with God in all three places: before God, before family, and before the church. There can be no separation between the man people see and the man God sees.

A holy man doesn't wear masks. He confesses quickly, repents sincerely, and walks consistently. He doesn't seek perfection—he seeks to be the same man at church, at home, and when he's alone.

Application:

• Evaluate your private habits—what would change if they were made public?

• Ask a trusted friend to hold you accountable in areas of personal holiness.

• Begin each day with a prayer for integrity and consistency.

Reflection Questions:

• Are there gaps between who I am in public and in private?

• Do I make room for secret sin, thinking it won't affect my witness?

• What does God see when no one else does—and what needs to change?

This Week's Brick:

This week, ask yourself one accountability question each night: Did I honor Christ when no one else was looking?

Give Yourself Grace:

God is not keeping score to punish you—He's watching your heart because He loves you. Your private moments matter, and grace is there to restore you every time.

Prayer:

Lord,

I don't want to pretend. Help me live with integrity before You and others. Make me the same man in secret that I am in public. Where I've hidden sin, bring it to light. Cleanse me. Guide me by truth. Let my life speak clearly of Your holiness. In Jesus' name, Amen.

CHAPTER 26
SURRENDER IS THE PATH TO STRENGTH

Scripture:

"Submit yourselves therefore to God. Resist the devil, and he will flee from you."
— James 4:7

Biblical Insight:

Strength begins at surrender. The world tells men to fight harder, push forward, take control. But Scripture tells us to submit—to bring our lives under God's rule before we attempt to stand against the enemy.

James 4:7 links victory over the devil with surrender to God. You cannot resist darkness if you're still holding onto your own will. You won't find power until you let go of pride.

Surrender is not passivity—it is spiritual alignment. It is choosing God's way over your impulses. It's laying down your preferences and picking up your cross.

A surrendered man prays first, listens long, obeys quickly, and lives humbly. He knows that his strength is not found in dominance—but in dependence.

Application:

•Start your day by saying aloud: "Lord, I surrender this day to You—my time, my words, my decisions."

•Identify one area you've been holding back from God—confess it and yield it.

•Practice obedience quickly—even when it costs you something.

Reflection Questions:

•What part of my life am I still trying to control instead of surrendering?

•Have I confused independence with godliness?

•How would my spiritual battles change if I lived fully under God's authority?

This Week's Brick:

This week, identify one area of your life you've been holding back from God. Write it down. Pray over it. Then surrender it in prayer—out loud.

Give Yourself Grace:

Surrender is not a sign of weakness—it's the gateway to strength. If you've clung too tightly, God isn't disappointed. He's inviting you to trust Him more deeply.

Prayer:

Lord,

I surrender. I yield my will, my plans, and my strength to You. Help me to live under Your authority every day. Teach me that obedience is not weakness but power. Let my life reflect trust—not resistance. And when the enemy comes, may he find me already submitted to the only true King. In Jesus' name, Amen.

CHAPTER 27
SAY NO TO THE FLESH, YES TO THE SPIRIT

SCRIPTURE:

"This I say then, Walk in the Spirit, and ye shall not fulfil the lust of the flesh."
— Galatians 5:16

Biblical Insight:

You cannot walk in two directions at once. Galatians 5:16 draws a clear line: when you walk in the Spirit, you will not fulfill the desires of the flesh.

The Christian life is not just about avoiding sin—it's about actively pursuing the Spirit's leadership. Saying "no" to the flesh is only possible when you say "yes" to the Spirit.

We as men are called to daily dependence on God. You emphasized that biblical manhood is Spirit-led, not self-led. The flesh calls you toward anger, lust, laziness, pride, and fear. The Spirit leads you to love, patience, purity, humility, and courage.

You do not win the battle by willpower. You win by surrender. The flesh never rests—but the Spirit never fails.

Application:

•Start each day by asking the Holy Spirit to guide your steps and guard your mind.

•When temptation comes, don't reason with it—replace it. Speak Scripture. Pray. Walk away.

•Feed the Spirit by spending focused time in the Word, prayer, and worship.

Reflection Questions:

•Where am I consistently giving in to the desires of the flesh?

•Do I rely more on discipline or on the Spirit when I'm tempted?

•What would change if I lived each moment fully yielded to the Spirit of God?

This Week's Brick:

Each morning this week, ask the Holy Spirit to lead your decisions. When temptation hits, whisper this prayer: "Lord, help me say yes to You."

Give Yourself Grace:

You won't win every battle—but you are not in the fight alone. The Spirit empowers what your flesh cannot accomplish. God is not grading your willpower; He's offering His presence.

Prayer:

Holy Spirit,

I need Your power today. My flesh pulls me away from what is right, but You draw me toward holiness. Help me walk in Your strength. Teach me to say no to temptation and yes to truth. Fill me, lead me, change me. Let my life reflect the victory You provide. In Jesus' name, Amen.

CHAPTER 28
HOLINESS IS A LIFELONG PURSUIT

SCRIPTURE:

"But as he which hath called you is holy, so be ye holy in all manner of conversation; Because it is written, Be ye holy; for I am holy." — 1 Peter 1:15–16

Biblical Insight:

God's standard has not changed—and neither has His calling. *"Be ye holy; for I am holy."* Holiness is not a phase or a project—it is the life-long pursuit of becoming like Christ in every area of life.

Peter reminds us that holiness is not optional for the believer. It touches every part of our "conversation"—our conduct, character, and choices. Holiness is not just about avoiding sin—it is about being set apart for God's glory.

Men must remember that spiritual growth takes time, focus, and intentionality. You don't drift into holiness. You pursue it—step by step, day by day, for the rest of your life.

Some days you'll struggle. Others you'll stumble. But if your eyes stay fixed on Christ, and your heart remains open to His Word, holiness will be the steady result.

Application:

• Reflect on one area of life where you've settled instead of striving for holiness.

• Commit to daily time in God's Word—feeding your soul and renewing your mind.

• Ask God to realign your goals—not toward success, but toward sanctification.

Reflection Questions:

• Have I treated holiness as optional, seasonal, or secondary?

• Where do I need to realign my life with God's standard of purity and devotion?

• How can I remain faithful in the long pursuit of becoming more like Christ?

This Week's Brick:

Set one spiritual goal this week—memorizing Scripture, confessing sin, or renewing a discipline. Track your progress and thank God for each step.

Give Yourself Grace:

You won't master holiness in a month—but you can grow today. If you've stalled, stumbled, or lost momentum, the journey isn't over. Get back up. God is still leading.

Prayer:

Father,

You are holy—and You've called me to follow You. Forgive me for every moment I've settled for less. I want to grow in purity, humility, and Christlikeness. Help me walk in holiness—not to earn Your love, but because I already have it. Shape me every day until I reflect more of You. In Jesus' name, Amen.

CHAPTER 29
FINISH CLEAN

SCRIPTURE:

"I have fought a good fight, I have finished my course, I have kept the faith." —
2 Timothy 4:7

Biblical Insight:

How you finish matters.

As Paul neared the end of his life, he didn't speak of comfort or applause—he spoke of faithfulness. He had fought well, stayed on course, and kept the faith. That is the goal of biblical manhood.

Finishing clean doesn't mean finishing without scars. It means finishing without quitting, without compromising, and without losing the fire that was there in the beginning.

Holiness is not an event—it's a journey. Temptation never retires. Sin doesn't take a season off. The need for watchfulness, repentance, humility, and grace never ends.

The legacy you leave is shaped by the choices you make today. If you want your children, church, and community to remember a man who walked with God—then finish clean. Keep your eyes on Christ. Stay faithful in your calling. And run with joy all the way to the end.

Application:

•Write down what you want your spiritual legacy to be—and live like it matters.

•Identify one area where compromise threatens your course—address it now.

•Ask a godly man near the finish line what kept him clean and close to Christ.

Reflection Questions:

•If I died today, what testimony would I leave behind?

•Am I coasting, drifting, or pressing forward in my walk with God?

•What will it take to finish strong—and finish clean?

This Week's Brick:

Reflect on your legacy this week. What do you want your children, wife, or brothers to say about your faith? Let that vision shape one decision you make today.

Give Yourself Grace:

Your past doesn't disqualify your future. You can finish clean, even if you started messy. Christ has already secured the victory—you just need to run your race with His strength.

Prayer:

Lord,

I want to finish well. I want to run my race with courage, fight the good fight of faith, and remain faithful to the end. Keep me from drifting. Guard me from compromise. Strengthen me to live each day with the end in view. And when I cross the finish line, may I hear, "Well done." In Jesus' name, Amen.

CHAPTER 30
HOPE THAT ENDURES

SCRIPTURE

"Now the God of hope fill you with all joy and peace in believing, that ye may abound in hope, through the power of the Holy Ghost."

—Romans 15:13

Biblical Insight:

The strength of a godly man is not just in what he endures—but in the hope he refuses to let go of.

Biblical hope is not wishful thinking. It's rooted confidence in who God is, what He has promised, and what He is still doing in you. When your family sees you respond to trouble with peace, to failure with humility, and to pain with trust, they are watching hope in action.

Hope reminds your children that God is bigger than what they fear. It tells your wife that Christ is near, even in weariness. And it speaks to your own soul when doubt and regret whisper loud.

You don't need every answer. But you need to know where to go. A man of God anchors his soul in the Word, bows in prayer, and rises again in grace.

When your life is shaped by hope, it gives your family something to hold on to—long after you're gone.

Real-Life Application:

• Share your salvation story with your children or spouse this week.

• Tell them where Christ met you and how He's still shaping you.

• When facing uncertainty, invite your family to pray with you for wisdom.

• Keep track of answered prayers and moments of God's help.

• Let them see that real hope rests in the faithfulness of God—not the strength of man.

This Week's Brick:

Ask your children or spouse, "Where do you need hope right now?"

Then pray with them for that specific burden—and follow up later in the week.

Share a story of hope with your child or someone younger in the faith. Let them hear how God brought you through.

Give Yourself Grace:

If your past holds more regret than inspiration, God can still use it. Every scar can become a testimony. Hope is not based on perfection—but on redemption.

Give Yourself Grace:

If your past is full of regret or inconsistency, do not despair.

God's hope is stronger than your history.

Even when you've fallen, He is not finished.

Every act of trust is a seed—planted in faith and watered by grace.

Let your family see a man who hopes in God, even when he's waiting.

Reflection Questions:

• Where do I need to trust God more deeply right now?

• What visible signs of hope does my family see in me?

• Have I shared my story of salvation and spiritual growth with my children?

Prayer

Heavenly Father,

Thank You for being the God of hope.

Thank You for saving me, for walking with me, and for never giving up on me.

Help me lead with hope, not fear. Let my life reflect Your joy and peace.

Give me the grace to point my family to You, especially when I fall short.

May my faith be steady, my heart surrendered, and my hope unshakable.

In Jesus' name, Amen.

CHAPTER 31
BECOMING THE STRONG MAN YOUR FAMILY NEEDS

Scripture:

"Watch ye, stand fast in the faith, quit you like men, be strong."

—1 Corinthians 16:13

Biblical Insight:

Biblical manhood is not a moment—it's a mission. A strong man isn't measured by worldly success, emotional suppression, or external bravado. He's shaped by surrender, forged in faith, and marked by consistency over time.

Throughout this journey, you've examined your heart, your home, your habits, your honor, and your holiness. None of these stand alone. Together, they form a life that points others to Christ. And that's the man your family truly needs.

Strong men do not rise by accident. They rise by decision—daily. They walk in humility, pursue discipline, speak with purpose, and finish clean. They fall sometimes. But they get back up.

You don't need to be remembered as perfect. You need to be remembered as faithful. Strong men leave scars of sacrifice, footprints of integrity, and a trail of grace behind them. They lead their homes by walking with Christ.

Let the strength you found in these pages take root—and let it grow into a legacy.

Real-Life Application:

• Reread your favorite devotional this week and apply it again.

• Identify one area—heart, home, habits, honor, or holiness—where God is still working on you.

• Make a 30-day commitment to grow deeper in that area.

• Share this journey with another man—invite him to walk with you.

• Pass the strength forward.

Reflection Questions:

• Which area—heart, home, habits, honor, or holiness—needs my renewed focus?

• What part of this journey do I need to revisit and deepen?

• Who can I walk alongside in this next season of growth?

This Week's Brick

Look back—then look ahead. Take one hour this week to reflect on what God has done in your heart through this journey. Then write a personal mission statement, or speak a blessing over your home, declaring the kind of man you intend to be from this point forward.

Simple Tip: Use one sentence each to describe how you will lead in heart, home, habits, honor, and holiness.

Give Yourself Grace

You won't get it all right. No man does. But you've shown up, day after day, asking God to shape you—and that matters more than you realize. If you've stumbled, missed days, or felt overwhelmed, grace still stands. God's strength is for men who know they need Him. Do not be discouraged. Be faithful. That's the legacy your family will remember.

Prayer:

Father,

Thank You for walking with me through this journey.

You know every failure, every step forward, and every place I still need to grow.

Give me strength to keep pursuing You, wisdom to lead my family, and grace to walk humbly.

Help me become the man You've called me to be—steadfast, surrendered, and strong.

In Jesus' name, Amen.

EPILOGUE

CLOSING CHARGE: WALK STRONG

You've read, reflected, and prayed through 31 days of truth. But this journey isn't over—it's just the beginning.

The strong men we need are not perfect, polished, or proud. They are present. They are growing. They are grounded in the Word of God and dependent on His grace.

Be that man.

Walk with integrity. Lead with love. Speak with wisdom. Forgive quickly. Pursue holiness. Keep building your heart, your home, your habits, your honor, and your hope.

The next generation is watching. Your family is counting on you. And your Heavenly Father is walking with you every step of the way.

Now go—and live the strength God has given you.